BIG ENGLISH 3

Mario Herrera • Christopher Sol Cruz

PUPIL'S BOOK

Contents

LIL	Writing	Phonics	I can...
...ence: Keeping clean ...teria, cough, decay, germs, healthy, ...sneeze ...en do you brush your teeth? ...ush my teeth (after) breakfast. ...ject: Keep it Clean poster	Sentence: Subjects and Verbs	**a_e, i_e, o_e** cake, face, game, shape bike, like, time, ride bone, home, note	...talk about what people do before and after school. ...talk about different times of the day. ...talk about keeping clean. ...find and use subjects and verbs.
...ial Science: Creative jobs ...nion designer, gallery, landscape, photographer, ...tch, upload ...en I paint, I feel happy. ...ject: Creative Job presentation	Sentence: Two Subjects and Verbs	**sm, st, sp, sk** smart, smile, smoke star, stop, storm space, Spain, spoon skates, ski, skin	...talk about what people do and where they work. ...talk about creative jobs. ...find and use two subjects and two verbs.
...ths: Pocket money ...ts, earn, euro, pocket money, subtotal, ...es, total ...cents times 4 equals 2 euros. ...w much do I earn? You earn two euros. ...ject: Chores Chart	Paragraph: Titles	**ay, oy** day, May, pay, ray, say, way boy, joy, soy, toy	...talk about how often people do things. ...talk about what people have to do. ...talk about chores and pocket money. ...use capital letters in titles.
...ence: Camouflage ...tom of the sea, camouflage, rock, stone, ...e bark ...called a (stonefish). ...ameleons) are found in deserts. ...ject: Animal Fact Sheet	Paragraph: Topic Sentences	**ea, oi, oe** bean, eat, meat, peach, sea, tea boil, coin, oil foe, toe	...talk about what animals can and can't do. ...talk about where animals are found. ...find and use topic sentences.
...ography: Climate ...rage, climate, extreme, opposite, temperature, ...rists ...a result of the temperature, few people ... there. ...w people live there because it is so hot. ...ject: Climate poster	Paragraph: Detail Sentences	**sc, sw, sn, sl** scar, scarf, scout swan, sweet, swim snack, snail, snow sleep, slim, slow	...talk about the weather today and in the past. ...talk about clothes. ...talk about climates around the world. ...find and use detail sentences.
...ence: Animal senses ...id, brain, danger, echo, information, tongues ...y taste with their tongues. ...hear, they use their legs. ...ject: Animal Senses poster	Paragraph: Final Sentences	**fl, pl, gl, bl** flag, flip-flops, fly plant, play, plum glad, glass, glow black, block, blow	...describe things by saying how they look, feel, taste, smell or sound. ...talk about the five senses in people and animals. ...find and use final sentences.
...ence: Vitamins ...od, bone, brain, energy, muscle, ..., teeth, vitamin ...amin A is good for our eyes. ... get Vitamin A from carrots. ...ject: Vitamin Plate	Paragraphs	**br, cr, dr, fr, gr, pr, tr** bread, brick cream, cry dream, drive frog, from grass, green train, troll	...ask and answer about food. ...talk about vitamins and how they help my body. ...find different parts of a paragraph.
...: Keeping healthy ...ive, activities, body, calorie, measure, put ...weight ...nning) is good for your (health). ...ject: Exercise Chart	Combining Sentences with *and*, *but*, *or*	**all, au, aw** all, ball, call, tall, wall haul, Paul claw, draw, law, yawn	...talk about healthy and unhealthy habits. ...ask and answer about activities in the past. ...use *and*, *or* and *but* in sentences.
...: Paintings ...autiful, boring, colourful, funny, interesting, ...ry, strange ... you like it? ..., I did. It was beautiful. ... you like it? ..., I didn't. It was scary. ...ject: Find out about a famous painting	Writing Sentences	**nt, ld, nd, st** ant, plant, tent child, cold , old band, hand, sand chest, fast, nest	...talk about actions in the past and places to visit. ...talk about paintings. ...make a paragraph.

Wake Up!

1:02

1 Listen, look and say.

Monday 13th May

1 wake up

2 eat breakfast

3 get dressed

4 go to school

5 go home

6 go to the park

7 play football

8 do my homework

9 play video games

10 watch TV

1:03

 2 Listen, find and say.

 3 Play a game.

4 **Listen and sing. Does Kate eat breakfast?**

Hurry, Kate!

It's Monday, 7:30.
Kate has to wake up.
Her mum sees the clock and says
Wake up sleepy head.

Go, go, go! Hurry, Kate!
Hurry, Kate! You can't be late!

Kate eats breakfast, she gets dressed.
It's 7:45.
It's time to go to school.
And she can't be late!

Chorus

Kate's got her backpack
And she's got her lunch.
What time is it now?
Oh, no, it's time to go!

Chorus

5 **Read, match and say. Ask and answer.**

1	7:00	**a**	seven forty-five
2	7:30	**b**	seven fifty-five
3	7:45	**c**	seven o'clock
4	7:55	**d**	seven thirty
5	4:45	**e**	five twenty-five
6	4:00	**f**	four forty-five
7	8:15	**g**	four o'clock
8	5:25	**h**	eight fifteen

When does she wake up?

She wakes up at seven o'clock.

 THINK BIG **Which activities do you do inside? Which do you do outside?**

6 **Listen and read. What does Luke do after school?**

1 Luke wakes up and goes into the kitchen.

2 Before school, Luke always eats breakfast.

3 After breakfast, he brushes his teeth. Then he washes his face.

4 He gets dressed.

5 He puts on his shoes. He's ready for school.

6 But there's no school today!

7 **Read and say** before school **or** after school.

1 Luke eats breakfast.
2 Luke gets dressed.
3 Luke plays football.
4 Luke puts on his shoes.
5 Luke wakes up.
6 Luke plays basketball.

THINK BIG **Do you like Mondays? Why/Why not?**
What different things do you do on different days?

1:08

8 Listen and look at the sentences. Help Luke and Amy make more.

get dressed do my homework

7:20 2:15 in the morning/afternoon/evening

When does he go to school ?

He goes to school at 8:10 .

When does she go home ?

She goes home in the afternoon .

9 Read and match. Make sentences with a partner.

1 Sam eats breakfast at 7:30
2 Jack wakes up at
3 Paula gets
4 Tim does his homework in
5 Sandra plays video
6 Alice watches

a games at 5:00 in the afternoon.
b in the morning.
c TV at 8:00 in the evening.
d dressed at 7:50 in the morning.
e 6:45 in the morning.
f the afternoon.

10 Look at 9. Ask and answer.

When does Paula get dressed?

She gets dressed at seven fifty.

11 **Listen and find the clocks.**

a

b

c

d

12 **What does Claudia do before and after school? Make sentences.**

Claudia's Schedule

6:30
wake up

3:20
go home

7:00
get dressed

6:45
get up

3:30
ride my bike

5:30
play football

4:45
do my homework

7:15
eat breakfast

6:30
eat dinner

7:30
go to school

13 **Look at 12. What does Claudia do in the morning, afternoon and evening?**

Claudia wakes up at 6:30 in the morning.

She plays football in the afternoon.

1:11

14 **Look, listen and repeat.**

> bacteria cough decay germs healthy ill sneeze

1:12

15 **Listen and read. What are bacteria?**

Keep It Clean!

Washing your hands, showering and brushing your teeth are three easy things you can do each day to keep yourself clean and healthy.

Have a shower

When your parents tell you to have a shower, they are giving you good advice. Wash your face, behind your ears and under your arms. Make sure you wash your whole body well. Use warm water and soap to wash away bacteria. Bacteria are tiny living things that can make you ill.

Brush your teeth

To keep your teeth strong and healthy, make sure you brush them twice a day. Brush them in the morning after breakfast. And brush them at night before you go to sleep. Brushing your teeth cleans away bacteria that can cause tooth decay. It's important to brush your teeth for two minutes.

Wash your hands

Every day, our hands pick up millions of germs that can make us ill. It's important to wash your hands with soap and water for at least 20 seconds. Wash your hands before you eat, after you go to the toilet, after you cough or sneeze and any other time your hands get dirty.

THINK BIG What other things can you do to stay healthy? Where can we learn about staying healthy?

16 **Read and say true or false.**

1 Have a shower to wash away bacteria.

2 Bacteria can make you ill.

3 Brush your teeth only once a day.

4 Brushing your teeth causes tooth decay.

5 Our hands pick up germs that make us healthy.

6 Wash your hands after you cough or sneeze.

17 **Ask and answer.**

> brush/teeth?   comb/hair?   have/shower?   take/bath?   wash/hands?

When do you brush your teeth?

I brush my teeth after breakfast and before I go to sleep.

PROJECT

18 **Make a Keep it Clean poster. Then present it to the class.**

Eat healthy food.

Brush your teeth after you eat sweets.

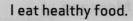

I eat healthy food.

1:13
19 Listen and read. It's twelve fifteen in Texas, what time is it in California?

Time Zones

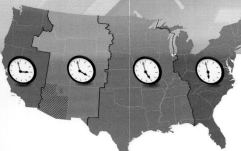

Do You Know What Time It Is?

Is it the same time everywhere in the world? No, it's not. That's because the world is divided into time zones. Look at the map of the United States. It's got four different time zones.

		two hours later	five more hours later
New York	It's 1:15 in New York and Manuel and his friends are finishing their lunch.	Now it's 3:15 in New York and school is over. Manuel is playing video games.	It's 8:15 at night now in New York and Manuel is finishing his homework.
Texas	In Texas, it's 12:15 and Maria is just finishing a Maths lesson.	In Texas, it's 2:15 and Maria is still in school.	In Texas, it's 7:15 and Maria is eating dinner.
Montana	John, in Montana, is hungry and is thinking about lunch. He looks at the clock. It's only 11:15 in the morning!	It's 1:15 in Montana and John is finishing his lunch.	In Montana, it's 6:15 now and John is playing basketball with friends.
California	And for Kara, in California, it's only 10:15 in the morning.	Kara, in California, looks at the clock and it's 12:15. Hooray! It's lunchtime!	In California, Kara is playing with her sister. It's 5:15.

20 Look at **19** and make false sentences, then correct.

> It's three fifteen and Manuel is playing football.

> No, he's playing video games.

THINK BIG It's ten o'clock in the morning where you are. Find out what time it is in Buenos Aires, Cairo and Sydney.

21 Read and find.

> A sentence has got a subject and a verb.
> She eats breakfast before school.

1 I ride my bike to school.

22 Find the subjects and verbs. Compare with your partner.

1 Andrew eats lunch at 12:30.
2 Marcia goes to school at 8:05.
3 We go home at 3:50 in the afternoon.
4 My brother does his homework at 4:30.
5 You eat dinner with your family in the evening.

23 What's missing, subject or verb? Make new sentences and compare with a partner.

1 Bridget 🔲 at 6:45 in the morning.
2 🔲 eats breakfast at 7:00.
3 Her 🔲 goes to the park with friends.
4 Beth 🔲 after school with her family.
5 🔲 get dressed in the morning.

24 Read about Jack's day. Change all the information in blue and red. Write a new paragraph.

Jack wakes up at six ten in the morning. He has a shower and gets dressed before school. He rides a bike to school and gets there at eight o'clock. His brother gets to school at eight ten. Jack plays football after school in the park. He does his homework at five fifteen. The family eat dinner together and then they watch TV.

25 Write four sentences about your day. Read them to your partner.

1:14

 26 **Listen, read and repeat.**

1 a_e   **2** i_e   **3** o_e

1:15

 27 **Listen and find. Then say.**

face   **b**ike   **b**one

1:16

 28 **Listen and blend the sounds.**

1 g-a-me   game   **2** c-a-ke   cake

3 t-i-me   time   **4** n-o-te   note

5 h-o-me   home   **6** sh-a-pe   shape

7 r-i-de   ride   **8** l-i-ke   like

1:17

 29 **Read aloud. Then listen and chant.**

What time is it?
It's time to play a game.
What time is it?
It's time to eat cake.
What time is it?
It's time to ride a bike.
What time is it?
It's time to go home.

30 **Choose the correct answer.**

When/What does Mia wake up on Friday? She **wakes/wake** up at seven fifteen because she has a shower, gets dressed, eats breakfast and brushes her teeth **before/after** school. She goes to school **at/in** eight o'clock. School finishes at three thirty in the **morning/afternoon**. When **do/does** she do her homework? At four fifteen. Then she goes **to/at** the park and **plays/playing** baseball with her friends.

31 **Make three sentences about things you do before school and three for after school.**

32 **Play the Silly Sentences game.**

6:15 in the evening

eat breakfast

Jack eats breakfast at six fifteen in the evening.

That's silly!

I Can

- talk about what people do before and after school.
- talk about different times of the day.
- talk about keeping clean.
- find and use subjects and verbs.

Lots of Jobs!

1:19

1 Listen, look and say.

Different Jobs

1 firefighter

2 police officer

3 cashier

4 waiter

5 farmer

6 scientist

7 nurse

8 student

1:20

2 Listen, find and say.

3 Play a game.

4 Listen and sing. How many jobs are in the song?

  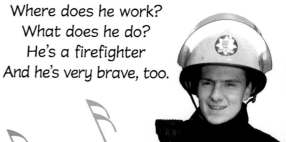

Working Together

There are many people
In our community.
So many jobs to do,
So many places to be.

Working together, working hard.
Nurse, farmer, teacher and chef.

Where does she work?
What does she do?
She's a nurse
And she always helps you.

Chorus

Where does he work?
What does he do?
He's a firefighter
And he's very brave, too.

5 Match the jobs in 1 to the places. Make sentences.

a
at a hospital

b
at a shop

c
at a fire station

d
at a university

e
at a laboratory

f
at a police station

g
at a restaurant

h
on a farm

 A student studies at a university.

A scientist works at a laboratory.

THINK BIG What job is this?
"I sometimes work at night. I sometimes work in the day.
I wear a uniform. I often work with another person."

Story

1:24

6 🎧 **Listen and read. What does Luke's mum do?**

1 Luke and his dad are at the hospital.

2 They want to find Luke's mum.

3 Luke's mum is at work.

4 Luke's mum works at the hospital.

5 Luke's mum isn't a doctor or a nurse.

6 Luke's mum is a cashier. She works at a shop. It's her birthday today!

7 **Read and complete the sentences. Then say.**

1 Luke is looking for his ❓ .

2 Luke's mum works at the ❓ .

3 Luke's mum isn't a doctor or a ❓ .

4 Luke's mum is a ❓ .

5 Today it's Luke's mum's ❓ .

THINK BIG What other people work in a hospital?
What do they do?
What do you think makes a good nurse?

Language in Action

8 **Listen and look at the sentences. Help Luke and Amy make more.**

1:25

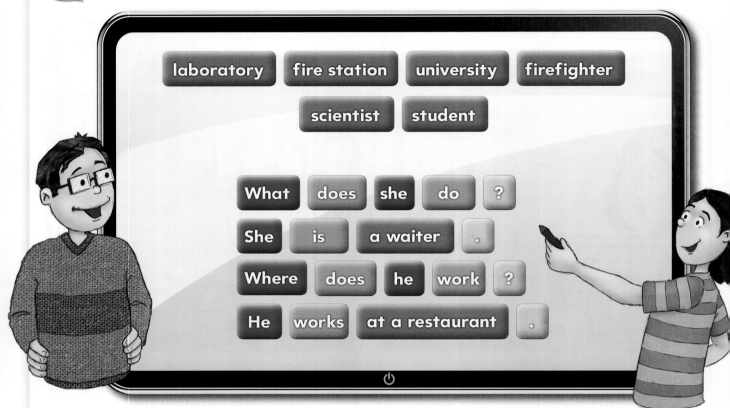

laboratory fire station university firefighter

scientist student

What does she do ?

She is a waiter .

Where does he work ?

He works at a restaurant .

9 **Put the dialogue in order with a partner. Then change the words in red and make new dialogues.**

a **She** works **at a school**.

b What does your **mum** do?

c **She's** a **nurse**.

d Where does **she** work?

10 **What about you? Ask and answer about your family.**

What does your dad do?

Where does he work?

He's a farmer.

He works on a farm.

20 Unit 2 language practice (*What does he do? He's a farmer.*)

1:27

11 Listen and match.

1 Megan

a

2 Susan

b

c

3 Ellie

12 Read and choose.

1 What/Why does your grandad do? He's a cashier and he works in a shop.

2 When/Where do Paul and Sally study? They study at university.

3 Where **do/does** Alice work? She works at a fire station.

4 What do you **do/does**? I'm a doctor.

5 I work **on/in** a farm. I'm a farmer.

6 We work **at/on** a hospital.

13 Look and make questions and answers.

1 a what/brothers/do?
   scientists
b where/work?
   laboratory
2 a what/you/do?
   teacher
b where/work?
   school
3 a what/mum/do?
   firefighter
b where/she/work?
   fire station

What do your brothers do?

They're scientists.

1:29

Look, listen and repeat.

> fashion designer gallery landscape photographer sketch upload

1:30

Listen and read. What does Susie do?

Creative Jobs

There are many kinds of jobs in the world. Some are creative. Would you like to do any of these jobs?

Artist

Jake Darley is an artist. When he paints, he uses paintbrushes, oil paints and an easel. He paints landscapes. "I like painting the beautiful mountains near my home. When I paint, I feel happy," he says. Jake shows his paintings in galleries and sells them to art collectors.

Photographer

Mark Portillo is a photographer. He takes photos of people and places all over the world. "When I travel, I always take my camera with me. I'm always looking for a good photo," he says. When Mark takes a photo, he uploads it to the computer. Then he sends his photos to websites, newspapers and television news programmes.

Fashion Designer

Susie Forester is a fashion designer. Susie says, "Designing clothes is fun. I get ideas from fashion shows, magazines and catalogues." When Susie's got an idea, she draws a sketch. Then she cuts a pattern and creates new clothes. "When I see people wearing my clothes, I feel really excited," she says.

THINK BIG **What other creative jobs can you think of?**
What qualities do you need to do a creative job?

16 **Correct the mistakes. Make new sentences.**

1 Jake Darley is a teacher.
2 Jake likes painting animals.
3 Mark Portillo is an artist.
4 When Mark takes a photo, he sends it to his mum.
5 Susie Forester is a nurse.
6 When Susie's got an idea, she writes a story.

17 **Look at 15. Make sentences.**

> I like painting. When I paint, I feel happy.

> You're an artist.

PROJECT

18 **Make a Creative Job presentation. Then present it to the class.**

Notes
• Michael Morpugo
• writes books for children
• tells stories
• feels happy

> Michael Morpugo is a writer. He writes books for children.

> He likes telling stories. When he tells stories, he feels happy.

1:31

19 Listen and read. Who helps tourists?

Making Communities Better

Here are three stories of kids working hard to make their communities better.

Lalana lives in Chiang Mai, Thailand. She knows that many schools in her city haven't got money to buy books. Lalana and her friends ask people to donate books. They take the books to schools in their city. Many schools have now got better books, thanks to Lalana and her friends.

Lalana

Carla lives in Barcelona, Spain. Many tourists visit Barcelona every year. Carla often sees people who are lost. At the weekends, Carla and her big sister help tourists find the places they are looking for. Carla likes helping people and she's proud of her city.

Carla

Marcus lives in a small town near Melbourne, Australia. Marcus walks to school every day. He sees a lot of rubbish along the road. Marcus and his friends have a contest every day. They pick up the rubbish and they see who can collect the most. They clean up the streets and they have fun.

Marcus

20 Read and say true or false.

1 Lalana buys new books to give to schools.
2 Carla and her sister help at the weekends.
3 Carla likes Barcelona.
4 Marcus and his friends do not enjoy picking up rubbish.

THINK BIG What could you do for your town or city? Brainstorm ideas together.

21 **Read and find.**

> A sentence can have two subjects and two verbs.
> Al is a farmer. Matt is a farmer.
> Al and Matt are farmers.
> I live in Rome. I work in Rome.
> I live and work in Rome.

1 Julie and John are students. They live and study at a university.

22 **Write the sentences. Use and to make two subjects or two verbs.**

1 I live in a town. I work in a town.

2 Lily is a scientist. Tom is a scientist.

3 My mother is a firefighter. My father is a firefighter.

4 I work at a restaurant. I eat at a restaurant.

5 My cousin lives in London. My cousin studies in London.

6 My sister lives on a farm. My brother lives on a farm.

23 **Complete the sentences for you. Then say.**

1 Before school, I 🔧 .   **2** After school, I 🔧 .

> Before school, I eat breakfast and get dressed.

> After school, I play football and do my homework.

1:32

24 **Listen, read and repeat.**

1 sm   **2** st   **3** sp   **4** sk

1:33

25 **Listen and find. Then say.**

smile   **stop**   **spoon**   **skates**

1:34

26 **Listen and blend the sounds.**

1	s-m-ar-t	smart	**2** s-k-i-n	skin
3	S-p-ai-n	Spain	**4** s-m-o-ke	smoke
5	s-k-i	ski	**6** s-t-or-m	storm
7	s-t-ar	star	**8** s-p-a-ce	space

1:35

27 **Read aloud. Then listen and chant.**

Stop and look.
Look at the stars,
The stars in space,
And smile!

1:37

28 Listen and say yes or no.

1 Julie's mum works at a hospital.

2 Her mum is a doctor.

3 Her dad is a student.

4 Her sisters work on a farm.

29 Make questions. Then say.

1 I'm a firefighter.

2 My brother works at a laboratory.

3 My dad is a police officer.

4 My two sisters are students.

5 My grandma works at a shop.

6 My uncles work at a hospital.

30 Play the Jobs game.

at a fire station
      hospital
      laboratory
      police station
      restaurant
      shop
      university
on a farm

Do I work at a hospital?   No.

I Can

- talk about what people do and where they work.
- talk about creative jobs.
- find and use two subjects and two verbs.

Working Hard!

1:38

1 Listen, look and say.

1 make my bed

2 walk the dog

3 practise the piano

4 take out the rubbish

5 do the dishes

6 clean my room

7 study for a test

8 feed the fish

1:39

2 Listen, find and say.

3 Play a game.

4 Listen and sing. What chores does Matt do?

Different Twins

My name's Matt
And my name's Mike.
We want to talk to you.
I do my chores
And I do, too.
But we are not alike.

Mike and Matt, Matt and Mike.
These two twins are not alike.

I'm Matt, I always clean my room.
I do my chores each day.
I sometimes do the dishes
And then we go and play.

Chorus

I'm Mike, I always make my bed.
I do my chores each day.
I sometimes walk the dog
And then we go and play.

Chorus

5 Use the chart to ask and answer questions about Matt.

Matt	Mon	Tue	Wed	Thu	Fri	Sat	Sun
clean his room	✓	✓	✓	✓	✓	✓	✓
feed the fish	✓		✓		✓	✓	✓
do the dishes				✓			✓
take out the rubbish							

Does Matt clean his room?

Yes, he does.

THINK BIG Which of these are your favourite chores?
Why are chores important?

6 **Listen and read. What time does Amy have to leave for school?**

I Have a Lot to Do

Hey, Amy...!

Yes? I'm busy!

1 Amy is thinking. Her mum comes into her bedroom.

You're always busy! What are you doing?

I have to do lots of things today. I'm making a list.

2 Amy likes making lists. She often makes a list of things she has to do.

What do you have to do?

I have to eat breakfast and brush my teeth. Then I have to feed the fish, clean my room and study for my Maths test.

3 Amy has to do lots of things before school.

I always leave at 7:50. Why?

What time do you have to leave for school?

4 Amy's clock still says 7:05.

5 What time does Amy have to leave? At 7:50? Oh, dear!

6 Amy's never late for school. She doesn't want to be late today!

7 **Read and say true or false.**

1 Amy has to do lots of things before school.
2 She has to eat breakfast.
3 She has to walk the dog.
4 She has to study for her English test.
5 She has to leave for school at 7:00.
6 She has to get a new alarm clock.

THINK BIG What kinds of lists do people make?
How do lists help us to remember things?
What other things help us to remember?

1:45

8 Listen and look at the sentences. Help Luke and Amy make more.

study for a test   do the dishes   make my bed

take out the rubbish

What   do we   have to do   ?

We   have to   practise the piano   .

What   does she   have to do   ?

She   has to   walk the dog   .

9 Follow the lines. What do they have to do?

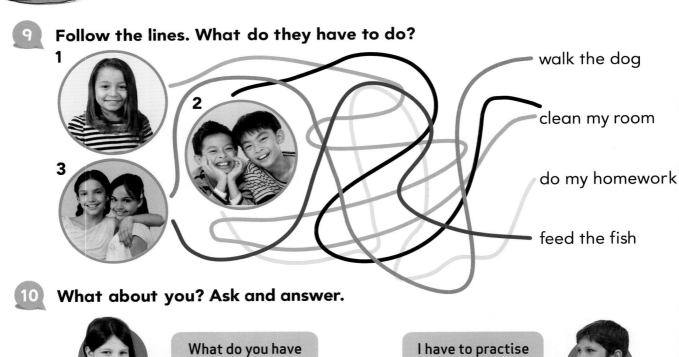

1

2

3

walk the dog

clean my room

do my homework

feed the fish

10 What about you? Ask and answer.

What do you have to do?

I have to practise the piano.

1:47

11 **Listen to Alexia's week and find the three mistakes.**

Monday	Tuesday	Wednesday	Thursday	Friday
do the dishes, practise the guitar	study for a test	take out the rubbish	make my bed	clean my room

12 **Put the words in order. Then say.**

1 sometimes | Do | make | your | bed? | you

2 do? | What | do | have | to | you

3 have | What | to | do? | Sally | does

4 never | the | dishes. | does | Jake

5 fish. | My | usually | feed | the | sisters

13 **Look at the chart. Make sentences about Leo. Use** always, usually, sometimes **and** never.

always ✶✶✶	usually ✶✶	sometimes ✶	never X

Leo's chores	Mon	Tue	Wed	Thu	Fri
study for a test	✓		✓		
clean his room	✓	✓	✓		✓
make his bed	✓	✓	✓	✓	✓
do the dishes					

14 Look, listen and repeat.

1:48

| cents   earn   euro   pocket money   subtotal   times   total |

1:49

15 Listen and read. How much pocket money does Anne earn?

Pocket Money

Lots of children around the world do chores to earn pocket money each week. Every week, Anne has to do lots of chores to earn pocket money.

Look at the chart to see the amount she gets for each chore:

 €1

	Amount (in euros)	Number of times a week (x)	Sub-total (in euros) (=)
do the dishes	50c	2	€1
clean my room	€1	3	€3
help cook dinner	€1	2	€2
take care of the pets	50c	2	€1
		Total:	€7

THINK BIG What other chores can you do to earn pocket money? Is it better to spend or save pocket money? Why?

16 **Look at the chart with a partner. Read and write the answers.**

1 If Anne cleans her room four times a week, how much pocket money does she earn?

2 If Anne helps to cook the dinner every day of the week, how much does she earn?

3 If she takes care of the pets on Monday, Tuesday, Wednesday and Thursday, how much does she earn?

4 If Anne wants to earn 10 euros, which chores does she have to do?

17 **Look at 15. Do the sums.**

One times five equals five.   **1 x 5 = 5**

I clean my room five times a week. How much pocket money do I earn?

That's right!

1 times 5 equals 5. You earn five euros.

PROJECT

18 **Make a Chores Chart. Then present it to the class.**

My pocket money			
	Amount	Number of times	Subtotal
make my bed	€1	4	€4
take out the rubbish			
feed my cat			

I earn 1 euro each time I make my bed. I make my bed four times a week. 1 times 4 equals 4. I get 4 euros.

1:50

19 Listen and read. Who does Chen Wei help?

Helping Out at Home

All around the world, kids help out at home. Listen to some of these kids' stories. Would you like to have to do their chores?

Chen Wei

My mother makes the best noodles and people come to her shop from all over Singapore to eat them. In the evening, her shop is very busy. After I do my homework, I help my mother cook noodles. We have fun cooking together. I love eating the noodles, too!

Ivan

I live on a goat farm in France. We get milk from the goats to make cheese. My family sell the cheese and I help take care of the goats. Every morning, I have to get up at 5 o'clock. I help my father feed the goats and get the milk. I go to school after I do my chores. It is hard work but I like helping my dad.

Leah

I live in Alaska. It always snows in winter. There's usually a lot of snow on the roads and the pavements. Everyone has to shovel snow. I shovel snow before I go to school every day. I don't mind — it's good exercise!

20 **Read and say** Ivan, Chen Wei or Leah.

1 I have to get up at five o'clock.

2 It snows a lot here.

3 My mother makes noodles.

4 Our family sell cheese.

5 I have to do my homework every day.

THINK BIG Which chores seem difficult and which seem easy? Why?

21 **Find the words we don't capitalize in the titles.**

Use capital letters for most words in titles.
Taking Care of a Big Dog

Good Things to Eat

My Brother and I

The Big Blue Car

A Day at the Park
with Grandma

To the Moon and Back

22 **Rewrite the titles. Use capital letters where necessary.**

1 helping my dad
2 lots of chores for my brother
3 helping out around the house
4 a strange day out
5 the jobs I like
6 helping my family is fun
7 my sister's new job

23 **How many English titles do you know?**
Write them with a partner.

1:51

24 **Listen, read and repeat.**

1 ay   **2** oy

1:52

25 **Listen and find. Then say.**

May

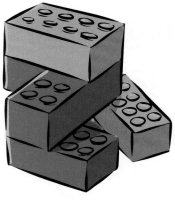

toy

1:53

26 **Listen and blend the sounds.**

1 d-ay   day   **2** j-oy   joy

3 s-ay   say   **4** p-ay   pay

5 b-oy   boy   **6** s-oy   soy

7 w-ay   way   **8** r-ay   ray

1:54

27 **Read aloud. Then listen and chant.**

What do we say?
It's May, it's May,
It's a nice day.
Come on, girls!
Come on, boys!
Bring your toys.

28 **Match. Then make statements for you. Use the words in the box.**

> always   have to   never   sometimes   usually

1	study for	**a**	dog
2	do	**b**	the piano
3	make	**c**	my room
4	walk the	**d**	a test
5	practise	**e**	the dishes
6	take out	**f**	the fish
7	feed	**g**	the rubbish
8	clean	**h**	pocket money
9	earn	**i**	my bed

29 **Copy the chart and complete for you. Then ask and answer.**

My Chores	Mon	Tue	Wed	Thu	Fri	Sat	Sun
clean my room							
do my homework							
do the dishes							
study for a test							

Do you always clean your room?

No, I don't. I always do my homework.

I Can

- talk about how often people do things.
- talk about what people have to do.
- talk about chores and pocket money.
- use capital letters in titles.

How Well Do I Know It? Can I Use It?

1 **Think about it. Read and draw. Practise.**

😊 I know this.　　😐 I need more practice.　　🙁 I don't know this.

		PAGES			
1	**Daily activities:** eat breakfast, go to school, practise the piano...	4, 28	😊	😐	🙁
2	**Telling time:** one o'clock, two thirty, 5:15...	5	😊	😐	🙁
3	**Jobs:** cashier, firefighter, nurse...	16	😊	😐	🙁
4	**Workplaces:** police station, restaurant, shop...	17	😊	😐	🙁
5	**When** does she get dressed? She gets dressed **at 7:00 in the morning**.	8	😊	😐	🙁
6	What does he do **before** school? He eats breakfast **before** school. What do you do **after** school? I watch TV **after** school.	9	😊	😐	🙁
7	What **does** he **do**? He **is** a cashier. Where **does** he **work**? He **works** at a shop.	20–21	😊	😐	🙁
8	What **do** they **have to** do? They **have to** feed the fish.	32	😊	😐	🙁
9	They **always** do their homework after school. She **usually** does the dishes. He **sometimes** takes out the rubbish. I **never** eat breakfast at 9:00.	33	😊	😐	🙁

1:56

2 **Get ready.**

A Complete the interview. Use the questions from the box. Then listen and check.

> What do you do before work?
> Where do you work?
> Do you eat dinner at home?
> When do you go to work?
> What do you do?

Katy: [1]

Max: I'm a chef.

Katy: Oh, really? [2]

Max: I work at a restaurant, the Pizza Palace.

Katy: I see. [3]

Max: I usually go to work at 2:00. I come home at 11:00 at night.

Katy: OK. [4]

Max: I have a shower, eat breakfast and get dressed. Then I feed my fish.

Katy: [5]

Max: No, I always eat dinner at the restaurant.

B Make more questions.

1 When ?

2 before work?

3 in the afternoon?

C Practise the dialogue in **A** with a partner. Include your new questions.

1
2
3
4
5
6
7
8
9

Get set.

 STEP 1 Choose a job.

 STEP 2 Write notes about your daily routine.

 STEP 3 Cut out the cards on page 121 of your Activity Book. Now you're ready to **GO!**

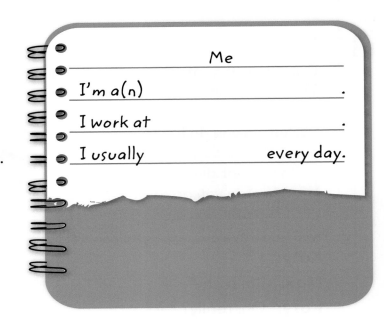

Me

I'm a(n) _____.

I work at _____.

I usually _____ every day.

 Go!

A Use the cards to make questions. Interview your partner. Write about your partner's daily routine. Then switch roles.

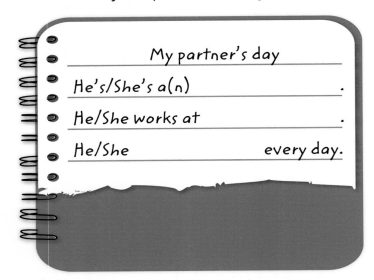

My partner's day

He's/She's a(n) _____.

He/She works at _____.

He/She _____ every day.

B Work in groups. Tell your classmates about your partner's daily routine.

Luisa always eats breakfast before school.

5 **Write about yourself in your notebook.**

- When do you wake up?
- What do you do before school?
- What chores do you have to do?
- What do you do after school?
- What time do you go to bed?
- What chores do you never do?

All About Me Date:

_____

_____

How Well Do I Know It Now?

6 **Think about it. Look at page 40 and your notebook. Draw again.**

A **Use a different colour.**

B **Read and think.**

I can start the next unit.

I can ask my teacher for help and then start the next unit.

I can practise and then start the next unit.

7 **Rate this Checkpoint.**

 very easy   easy   hard   very hard

 fun   OK   not fun

unit 4
Amazing Animals

2:01

1 Listen, look and say.

1 bear

2 deer

3 owl

4 camel

5 lizard

6 penguin

7 toucan

8 sea lion

9 shark

2:02

 2 Listen, find and say.

 3 Play a game.

4 **Listen and sing. How many birds are in the song?**

Animals are Amazing!

Animals are amazing!
We see them far and near.
Some live in forests
Like owls, bears and deer.

Some live in deserts
Like camels and some snakes.
Some live in water,
In oceans, seas and lakes.

Amazing, amazing animals
What can animals do?
They can fly, they can swim, they can jump!
We share the earth with you!

5 **Match the animals to places. Ask and answer.**

deserts forests ice and snow jungles
lakes mountains oceans rainforests

Where do lizards live?

Some live in deserts
and some in lakes.

THINK BIG **Look at the photos. Which is your favourite animal and why?**

Story

1 Luke and Amy are watching a sea lion show at the zoo.

2 Luke has to cover his ears.

3 The sea lion can balance a ball on its nose!

4 Then Luke and Amy watch a parrot show.

5 The parrot's name is Smartie.

6 When Smartie starts talking, Smartie can't stop!

 7 **Read and match. Make sentences.**

1 Sea lions can't   **a** stop talking.

2 Sea lions can   **b** parrot.

3 Smartie is a   **c** say its name.

4 Smartie can   **d** sing very well.

5 Smartie can't   **e** do great tricks.

 THINK BIG What other animals are very clever?
What can they do?
What different ways are there to learn about animals in a zoo?

8 Listen and look at the sentences. Help Luke and Amy make more.

climb trees   swim   run

camels   lizards   toucans

What | can | parrots | do | ?

Parrots | can | talk and fly | .

What | can | you | do | ?

I | can | talk but | I | can't | fly | ?

9 Make the questions with can. Then answer with a partner.

1 What/kangaroos/do?

2 What/monkeys/do?

3 What/deer/do?

4 What/crocodiles/do?

5 What/you/do?

10 Make statements. Then say true or false.

Elephants can run and fly.

False! Elephants can run but they can't fly.

2:09

11 **Copy the chart and complete. Listen and check. Then complete for you.**

	swim	fly	climb trees	run	?
bears					
camels					
sharks					
lizards					
?					

12 **Look at 11. Ask and answer.**

13 **Read the dialogue. What are the two animals? Now role play with a partner.**

A: Are you ready for an animal quiz?

B: Yes, I am!

A: OK. These animals live in ice and snow. They can swim but they can't fly.

B: I know. ¹ ?

A: Right! Now it's your turn.

B: OK. They live in forests. They can climb trees and swim.

A: Snakes?

B: No. They've got four legs and can run fast.

A: Oh, I know. ² ?

B: That's right!

2:10

14 **Look, listen and repeat.**

> bottom of the sea   camouflage   rock   stone   tree bark

2:11

15 **Listen and read. What can chameleons do?**

Animal Camouflage

Many animals blend in with their surroundings. This is called camouflage. Animals use colour, body shape or both to blend in. Camouflage helps animals to hide and find food.

Chameleons Change Colour

Chameleons are found in rainforests and in deserts. A chameleon can change its colour. On a brown rock in the desert, it can be brown. In a green tree in the rainforest, it can be green. Very cool!

chameleon

Polar Bears Hide in the Snow

Polar bears are found in the ice and snow. Everything around them is white. They are covered in white fur but their eyes, noses and the bottoms of their feet are black. It's not easy to see a polar bear in the snow.

polar bear

Animals Hide for Different Purposes

This fish is called the stonefish. It looks like stones on the bottom of the sea. It uses camouflage to get food. The fish it eats can't see it. If they touch the stonefish by mistake, it stings them to death and eats them. This frog is called the grey tree frog. It is found in the forests of North America. It uses camouflage to hide. It looks like a tree branch. The birds and snakes that eat grey tree frogs can't see them against the bark of the tree. Look at the pictures. Is it easy to see these animals?

stonefish

grey tree frog

THINK BIG **Can you think of any other animals that live in rainforests and deserts? What do they look like? What other animals live in the ice and snow? What do they look like?**

16 Read and say true or false.

1   A chameleon can look like trees or rocks.
2   A polar bear is found in the desert.
3   A stonefish isn't found on the bottom of the sea.
4   A grey tree frog looks like tree bark.

17 Look at the cards. Play a game.

name:
chameleon
found:
rainforests and deserts
camouflage:
looks like rocks and trees

name:
grey tree frog
found:
forests
camouflage:
looks like tree bark

name:
polar bear
found:
ice and snow
camouflage:
looks like snow

name:
stonefish
found:
bottom of the sea
camouflage:
looks like stones

It's found on the bottom of the sea. It looks like stones.

It's called a stonefish.

PROJECT

18 Make a Fact Sheet about an animal that uses camouflage. Then present it to the class.

The sidewinder snake

Name:
sidewinder snake

Found:
in the desert in North America

Camouflage:
hides in the sand / looks like sand

This is called a sidewinder snake. It is found in deserts. It uses camouflage to hide in the sand. It's brown and it looks like sand.

2:12

19 **Listen and read. How many pet cats are there in America?**

Pets in Different Places

Many people around the world have got pets. In the United States, Canada and the United Kingdom, cats are very popular. In the United States, there are about 93 million pet cats.

Cats and other animals are popular pets in other countries, too. But there are lots of different pets around the world. Many people in China have got goldfish as pets.

In Mexico, birds such as parakeets are also popular. Parakeets are colourful. They like to play with people and they can talk! In Italy, many people have got canaries. Canaries can sing all day!

There are many different kinds of pets. Rabbits, hamsters and snakes are also very popular around the world. What kind of pet do you like?

20 **Read and answer the questions.**

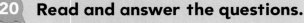

1 How many cats are there in America?

2 What is a popular pet in China?

3 What is a parakeet?

4 What's the name of the bird people in Italy have got as pets?

 THINK BIG **Do you think a snake is a good pet? Why/Why not?**

2:13

21 **Listen and read. What's Spotty like?**

title ⟶

topic sentence ⟶

My Favourite Pet

by Aaron Michaels

My favourite pet is my snake, Spotty. He is a corn snake. He is 50 centimetres long and he is red and white. I feed him one small mouse every week. He is friendly. He does not bite people. Some people don't like snakes but snakes can make good pets.

22 **Read 19 again. Find the first topic sentence.**

> A topic sentence gives the main idea in a paragraph.

23 **Read and match the titles with the topic sentences.**

Title	Topic Sentence
1 A Day at the Zoo	**a** My sister and I have got many pets at home.
2 My Mother's Job	**b** My favourite time of day at school is Art class.
3 My Favourite Class	**c** I have to do lots of chores at home after school.
4 After-School Jobs	**d** My mother is a chef at an Italian restaurant.
5 Our Pets	**e** When I go to the zoo, I spend the whole day there.

24 **What is your favourite animal? Write a title and a topic sentence.**

2:14

 25 **Listen, read and repeat.**

1 ea   **2** oi   **3** oe

2:15

 26 **Listen and find. Then say.**

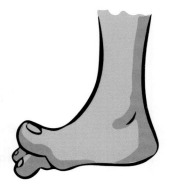

eat   **coin**   **toe**

2:16

 27 **Listen and blend the sounds.**

1 s-ea   sea   **2** b-oi-l   boil
3 b-ea-n   bean   **4** t-ea   tea
5 p-ea-ch   peach   **6** m-ea-t   meat
7 oi-l   oil   **8** f-oe   foe

2:17

 28 **Read aloud. Then listen and chant.**

So, Joe, boil the beans,
Add the oil,
Add the meat.
Eat the beans,
Eat the meat,
Eat the peach
And drink the tea.

29 Find the animals. Make sentences about where each animal is found.

1 wol

2 karsh

3 esa noil

4 reab

5 reed

6 zardil

An owl is found in forests.

30 Complete the dialogue. Then ask and answer.

Daniel: Where do sharks live?

Teresa: ¹ 🔮 .

Daniel: Right. ² 🔮

Teresa: Camels live in the desert.

Daniel: Right again! ³ 🔮

Teresa: Camels can walk and run a little but they can't jump or fly.

Daniel: How about penguins? Can they swim and fly?

Teresa: ⁴ 🔮

Daniel: That's right!

31 Make sentences about toucans and sea lions.

What can they do?

What can't they do?

Where are they found?

I Can

- talk about what animals can and can't do.
- talk about where animals are found.
- find and use topic sentences.

Wonderful Weather!

2:19

1 Listen, look and say.

1 It's windy.

2 It's cold and snowy.

The **Weather** today

hot

warm

cool

cold

3 It's cool and cloudy.

4 It's hot and sunny.

5 It's warm and rainy.

2:20

2 Listen, find and say.

3 Play a game.

4 Listen and sing. What's the weather like today?

Cool Weekend!

What's the weather like today?
Rainy, sunny, hot or cold?

On Sunday, it was rainy,
It was very cold, too.
I was nice and warm in my winter coat,
Outside the sky wasn't blue!

Now it's Monday. It's sunny.
Great! I can go out and play.
Oh, no! I have to go to school.
Never mind! The weekend was cool!

Chorus (x2)

2:23

5 Listen and find. Then ask and answer for you.

> What do you wear on sunny days?

> On sunny days, I wear shorts, a T-shirt and sunglasses.

THINK BIG **What weather is good for...**
a football practice? **b** a walk in the park?
c going to the beach? **d** going skiing?

6 Listen and read. Where is Amy going today?

Amy is Ready!

I'm ready for my hike. I've got my hiking boots, water and snacks.

1 Amy is happy. Today her class is going on a hike.

Wait a minute! You need your raincoat and umbrella.

Why? What's the weather like? Is it rainy?

2 Mum doesn't think Amy is ready.

No, not right now but what was the weather like yesterday?

It was rainy.

3 Mum doesn't want Amy to get wet.

And last night, it was cold and windy. Take your jumper. And your hat and gloves, too.

OK...

4 She doesn't want Amy to get cold.

5 Amy isn't worried about the weather.

6 Amy is ready for all kinds of weather!

7 **Look at the story. Answer the questions with a partner.**

1 What's Amy's class doing today?
2 What was the weather like yesterday?
3 What was the weather like last night?
4 What's the weather like today?
5 What's Amy wearing at the end of the story?

THINK BIG Do you think it's a good idea for Amy to take so many clothes?
What clothes would you take?

8 Listen and look at the sentences. Help Luke and Amy make more.

2:26

| cold | windy | cloudy |

What | is | the weather like | today | ?

It | 's | warm and sunny | now | .

What | was | the weather like | yesterday | ?

It | was | rainy and cold | .

I | wasn't | hot | .

We | weren't | warm | last Sunday | .

9 Look at the weather chart. Answer the questions.

M	T	W	Th	F

1 Today is Monday. What's the weather like today?
2 Today is Tuesday. What's the weather like today?
3 It's sunny. What day is it today?
4 It's windy. What day is it today?
5 Today is Thursday. What was the weather like yesterday?

10 Ask and answer.

I'm wearing a T-shirt, shorts and sandals. What's the weather like?

It's sunny and warm.

11 **Read and find the correct sentence and say. Correct for you.**

1 It is sunny yesterday.
It was sunny yesterday.

2 Today it's snowy.
Yesterday it's snowy.

3 It's cool and windy now.
It was cool and windy now.

4 It was rainy last night.
It is rainy last night.

5 We aren't warm last Sunday.
We weren't warm last Sunday.

6 She isn't cold today.
She wasn't cold today.

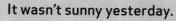

It wasn't sunny yesterday.

12 **Complete the role-play with is or was. Then say with your partner.**

Becky: My holiday is great fun. Yesterday, ¹ 🔲 great! I ² 🔲 at the beach all day!

George: Wow! What ³ 🔲 the weather like yesterday?

Becky: It ⁴ 🔲 hot and sunny. What ⁵ 🔲 the weather like at home today?

George: It ⁶ 🔲 cool and rainy.

13 **Put the temperatures in order. Start with cold. Make sentences about what you are wearing.**

cold   cool   hot   warm

It's cold today. I'm wearing boots, trousers, a jumper, coat and gloves.

2:28

14 Look, listen and repeat.

> average   climate   extreme   opposite   temperature   tourists

2:29

15 Listen and read. What does climate mean?

What's the Weather Like?

The year-round weather in a place is called its climate. In some places, the climate is the same all year long – and it can be extreme.

Wow! That's Hot!

There are many hot places on the planet but the Lut Desert in Iran is super hot. The temperatures there can be 70 degrees Celsius! It is so hot that not many people go there. As a result, the Lut Desert is also a very quiet place.

It's Freezing!

Oymyakon, Russia, is the opposite of the Lut Desert. It is very cold. There is lots of snow and temperatures can be minus 70 degrees Celsius. Not many people live in Oymyakon because of the cold.

I'm Thirsty!

The Atacama Desert in Chile is dry. In some parts of this desert, it never rains at all. As a result, not many people live there. But tourists go to see this very beautiful place. People say the Atacama Desert looks like the moon.

Where's My Umbrella?

It rains almost every day in Lloró, Colombia. Lloró gets an average of 13 metres of rain every year. That's a lot of rain! The trees grow very quickly because of the rainy climate.

THINK BIG What would it be like to live in one of these places? What's the climate like where you live?

16 **Read again and answer.**

1 Why do not many people go to the Lut Desert?
2 What is the result of so few people going there?
3 How cold can it get in Oymyakon?
4 Why is the Atacama Desert so dry?
5 Why do the trees grow quickly in Lloró?

17 **Use the chart. Ask and answer.**

Place	Climate	Weather	Effect
desert	hot and dry	never rains	not many plants grow there
			not many animals live there
rainforest	hot and wet	always rains	plants and trees grow quickly
mountains	cold and snowy	usually snows	lots of tourists visit

What's the weather like in the desert?

It's hot and dry because it never rains. As a result, not many plants grow there.

PROJECT

18 **Make a Climate poster. Then present it to the class.**

The Canadian Arctic

The Canadian Arctic is very cold and snowy. In winter, temperatures can be minus 50 degrees Celsius. As a result, many animals sleep all winter.

2:30

19 **Listen and read. What is popular in Japan?**

All-Weather Sports

Children around the world enjoy outdoor sports. In the United States, many children play baseball. In India and England, cricket is a popular game. And football is loved by children all over the world. But when the weather is bad, it's not much fun to play any of these sports. So what can you do? Kids in other parts of the world just might have the answer.

Flying High

If it's too windy, it can be difficult to play football and some other outdoor sports. But one thing many kids know is that a windy day is great for flying a kite. Children all over the world enjoy being outdoors and flying kites but it is very popular in Japan and other Asian countries.

Fun in the Water

In parts of Africa, it is dry for many months of the year. But when the rain comes, the dry rivers and lakes fill up quickly. Kids love it. They go swimming and play games in the water. It's a fun time for everyone when it rains.

Sledging

In Alaska and parts of Canada, it snows a lot. But that doesn't stop kids from having fun outdoors. When it snows, they wear warm clothes and go outside. They often go sledging. Some kids also do an interesting sport called dog sledging. Dogs pull the sledge and the kids ride on it. So turn off the TV. Even if it is windy, wet or cold, there are lots of fun things to do outside.

20 **Look at 19. Say the sports.**

1 This is a popular sport in England.

2 On a windy day, this is great fun.

3 When it rains a lot, you can do this in the lake.

4 You can do this when it snows a lot.

THINK BIG **Think about sports you play or sports you know. Which ones are good for...**

a hot, sunny days?   **b** wet, rainy days?   **c** snowy days?

21 **Read. Then choose.**

Here is a topic sentence.

My favourite season is summer.

After the topic sentence, we give more information with detail sentences.

In the summer where I live, the weather is usually sunny and hot. I like going to the beach with my friends. We swim or play volleyball.

detail sentence   topic sentence

1 A ? tells us what the paragraph is about.

2 A ? gives us more information.

22 **Read the topic sentence below. Which sentences give details about this topic?**

Topic sentence: *Winter is my favourite time of year.*

1 We like building snowmen in winter, too.

2 It's not cold in summer.

3 My friends and I like to go sledging.

4 We usually wear hats and gloves in winter.

5 My sister's favourite season is spring.

6 It's cold and snowy in winter but I like it.

Writing Steps

23 **Write about your favourite season.**

1 Choose your favourite season.

2 Write a title.

3 Write a topic sentence.

4 Write three detail sentences.

2:31

24 **Listen, read and repeat.**

1 SC　　　　**2** SW　　　　**3** sn　　　　**4** sl

 2:32

25 **Listen and find. Then say.**

scarf　　　　**sweet**　　　　**snail**　　　　**sleep**

 2:33

26 **Listen and blend the sounds.**

1 s-c-ou-t　scout　　　　**2** s-n-a-ck　snack
3 s-w-i-m　swim　　　　**4** s-l-i-m　slim
5 s-n-ow　snow　　　　**6** s-w-a-n　swan
7 s-l-ow　slow　　　　**8** s-c-ar　scar

 2:34

27 **Read aloud. Then listen and chant.**

A slow snail is eating a snack
And a slim swan is swimming.

28 Look at the weather reports. Complete the questions and answers.

Barcelona, Spain	
Yesterday	Today
Temperature: 33 °C	Temperature: 28 °C

Glasgow, Scotland	
Yesterday	Today
Temperature: 4 °C	Temperature: 12 °C

1 What/weather/Barcelona/yesterday?

2 Yesterday, in Barcelona it was ❓ .

3 What/weather/Barcelona/today?

4 Today, it's ❓ .

5 What/weather/Glasgow/yesterday?

6 ❓

7 What/weather/Glasgow/today?

8 ❓

 29 Find the differences. Talk with a partner.

Picture 1

Picture 2

 In Picture 1, it's hot and sunny.

In Picture 2, it's cold and snowy.

30 Choose one picture from 29. Write a topic sentence and three detail sentences.

I Can

- talk about the weather today and in the past.
- talk about clothes.
- talk about climates around the world.
- find and use detail sentences.

Smells Good!

2:36

1 Listen, look and say.

1 This music sounds lovely.

2 This band sounds awful.

3 This soup tastes horrible.

4 This pie tastes delicious.

Senses

5 This apple tastes sweet.

6 These flowers smell nice.

7 My hair looks terrible.

8 My jumper feels soft.

9 These shoes feel tight.

2:37

2 Listen, find and say.

3 Play a game.

4 Listen and sing. Where do the girls like going?

Grandma's House

We love my Grandma's house.
It always smells so nice.
It smells like ginger cookies
Sweet, with a little spice!

**Yummy smells and her smiling face.
We really love my Grandma's place.**

Grandma likes playing old songs
From when she was very young.
The music sounds so wonderful,
We have to sing along.

We always do my favourite thing
Baking ginger cookies.
They taste so nice and yummy,
We are both very lucky!

Chorus

5 Match the pictures to the words. Then ask and answer about **1.**

 **1**

 **2**

 **3**

 **4**

 **5**

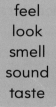
feel
look
smell
sound
taste

This pie tastes delicious.

Number 4.

THINK BIG Can you think of other things you describe with these adjectives?
sweet   tight   lovely   horrible

6 2:41 **Listen and read. What kind of soup does Luke try?**

1 Luke smells something bad coming from the kitchen.

2 It *is* fish soup. Luke thinks it smells horrible.

3 Amy tries the soup.

4 Luke tries the soup.

5 Luke thinks the soup tastes awful.

6 Amy has got a cold. That's why she can't taste the soup.

7 Put the sentences in order.

a Amy thinks the soup tastes OK.

b Luke thinks the soup tastes terrible.

c Luke thinks the fish soup smells awful.

d Amy tries the soup.

e Luke tries the soup.

f Luke asks Amy to try the soup.

THINK BIG **Which senses do we use when we are...**
a in a restaurant?   b at a football match?
c at school?

How do our senses make us aware of danger?

2:42

8 Listen and look at the sentences. Help Luke and Amy make more.

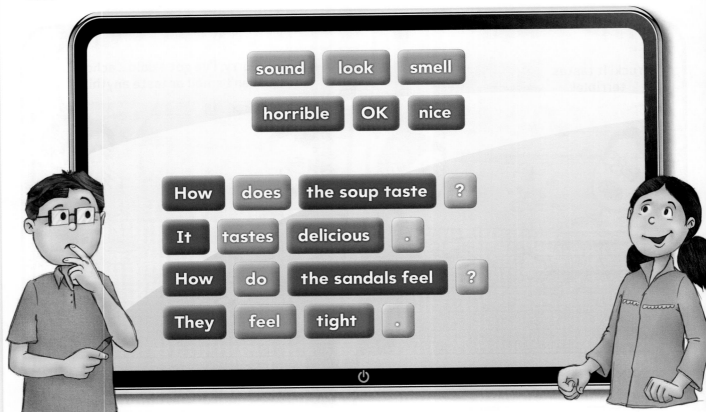

sound | look | smell

horrible | OK | nice

How | does | the soup taste | ?

It | tastes | delicious | .

How | do | the sandals feel | ?

They | feel | tight | .

2:43

9 Are the adjectives positive or negative? Copy and complete.
Then listen and check.

amazing awful bad delicious good horrible lovely nice terrible

Positive	Negative
amazing	awful

10 **Read and choose. Complete the answers.**

awful   good   great   nice   soft

1 A: How do these flowers **smell/smells**?
   B: ❓ .

2 A: How does my new shirt **look/looks**?
   B: ❓ . I like the colour.

3 A: How does the sandwich **taste/tastes**?
   B: ❓ . I don't like tomatoes!

4 A: How does the school band **sound/sounds**?
   B: ❓ . They practise every day.

5 A: How do your new gloves **feel/feels**?
   B: ❓ .

11 **Complete the questions.**

1 ❓ the guitar music sound?
2 ❓ the flowers smell?
3 ❓ my hair look today?
4 ❓ that pizza taste?
5 ❓ the shoes feel?

12 **Ask and answer. Use the words in the boxes.**

delicious   horrible   great   lovely   soft   tight

apples   flowers   hat   music   trousers

How does the music sound?

It sounds lovely.

2:45

13 Look, listen and repeat.

avoid   brain   danger   echo   information   tongues

2:46

14 Listen and read. How do lizards smell things?

Our Senses Keep Us Safe

Every minute of every day, our senses get information and send it to the brain. We use this information to understand the world around us. Our senses tell us whether food is good and fresh or bad and rotten and whether something is hot or cold. Our senses help to keep us safe.

Like people, animals use their senses to find food and avoid danger. But many animals' senses are different from people's senses.

Did you know?

- Some animals, such as snakes and lizards, don't smell with their noses. They smell with their tongues!
- Chameleons have got very long, sticky tongues. They use their tongues to catch their food and to taste it!
- Butterflies and some other insects taste things with their legs.

- Bats' eyes cannot see well. To 'see' things, they make a sound and listen for the echo. They can 'see' how big something is and find it.

THINK BIG Why do animals use their senses differently to people? Which sense is the most important? Why?

15 **Read and match. Make sentences.**

1 People and animals
2 Snakes and lizards smell
3 Chameleons use their tongues
4 Butterflies taste
5 To 'see' things bats use

a to catch food and taste it.
b with their legs.
c their ears.
d with their tongues.
e need their senses to be safe.

16 **Play a game.**

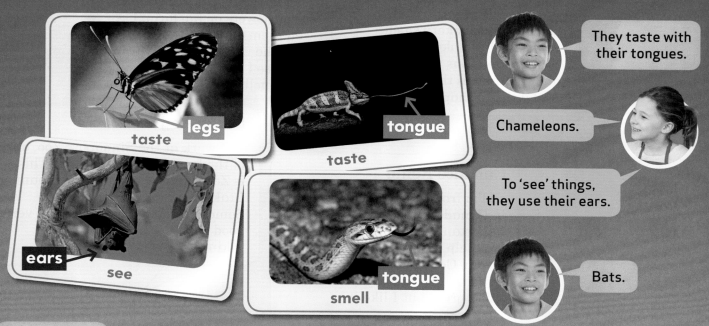

taste **legs**

tongue
taste

ears see

tongue
smell

They taste with their tongues.

Chameleons.

To 'see' things, they use their ears.

Bats.

PROJECT

17 **Find out about other animal senses. Then present it to the class.**

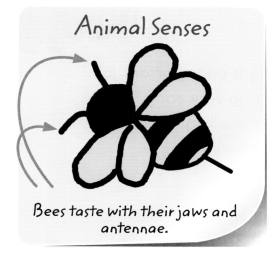

Animal Senses

Bees taste with their jaws and antennae.

Bees use their senses differently to people.

2:47

18 Listen and read. Who likes making people happy?

How Does Your Job Smell?

André Tyrode

I live in Lyon, France. I'm a baker. I get up early every day and make pastries. Of course, everything I make tastes good. But the bakery smells wonderful! It makes people want to share delicious treats together and that makes them happy. And if they're happy, I'm happy!

Alberto Rivera

I'm from Costa Rica. I grow flowers on my farm. I sell them and send them all over the world. I like my job because I can look at flowers and smell them all day!

Candace Reilly

I'm from Calgary, a city in Canada. My job is very important. I pick up rubbish and help keep my city clean. Today, Calgary is the cleanest city in Canada! My job doesn't smell great but I like it.

Sarah Ang

I work at the Singapore Zoo, one of the best zoos in the world. This is Zelda. She is an Asian elephant. I take care of Zelda at the zoo. Sometimes Zelda doesn't smell very good so I give her a bath! I like taking care of animals.

19 Read **18** and find who says what.

1 I work on a farm.

2 I've got an important job.

3 I work with animals.

4 I get up very early.

5 Baking makes me feel happy.

6 I like smelling flowers.

7 When she doesn't smell nice, I give her a bath.

8 I like my job.

THINK BIG Which job sounds interesting to you?
What's your favourite smell? Why?

20 **Read and complete with** topic sentence, detail sentences **and** final sentence.

A paragraph begins with a ¹ ？ . It introduces the subject of the paragraph.

I love tomatoes.

² ？ expand on your topic by giving details about it.

Home-grown tomatoes taste delicious and they are good for you.

Fresh tomatoes right from the garden smell great.

They look nice in a salad, too.

You end your paragraph with a ³ ？ . It expresses the same idea as your topic sentence but in a different way.

Of all fruits and vegetables, tomatoes are my favourite.

21 **Read the paragraphs. Find the best** final sentence **for each one.**

1 Topic Sentence: My favourite toy is my teddy bear, Simpson.

Detail Sentences: Simpson is very old. He doesn't look very nice. But I like him very much. He feels soft and he always smells so nice. He can't talk or run but that's OK.

Final Sentence:
a Simpson is just an old teddy bear.
b I love Simpson more than any of my other toys.
c Simpson doesn't do a lot.

2 Topic Sentence: My favourite teacher is Mrs Graham.

Detail Sentences: Mrs Graham is very nice. She teaches us many interesting things. She never gets angry. Mrs Graham is friendly and she smiles a lot.

Final Sentence:
a Mrs Graham is 40 years old.
b Mrs Graham doesn't like cake very much.
c Mrs Graham is the best teacher at our school.

22 **Write a** final sentence **for this paragraph.**

Autumn is my favourite season. The colourful leaves on the trees look so pretty. The air feels nice and cool and autumn smells great.

2:48
23 Listen, read and repeat.

1 fl   **2** pl   **3** gl   **4** bl

 2:49
24 Listen and find. Then say.

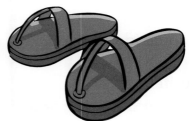   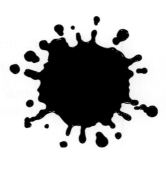

flip-**fl**ops   **pl**um   **gl**ass   **bl**ack

 2:50
25 Listen and blend the sounds.

1 f-l-a-g   flag   **2** p-l-a-n-t   plant

3 p-l-ay   play   **4** f-l-y   fly

5 g-l-a-d   glad   **6** g-l-ow   glow

7 b-l-o-ck   block   **8** b-l-ow   blow

2:51
26 Read aloud. Then listen and chant.

It's summer.
Yellow plums,
Green plants.
Flip-flops,
Black shorts,
It's summer.
I'm glad!

27 Look at the pictures. Complete the questions. Then say.

1 How does the ice cream 🔖 ?
2 How does the rock band 🔖 ?
3 How does the man 🔖 ?
4 How does the stuffed animal 🔖 ?
5 How do the flowers 🔖 ?

28 Make the answers for **27**.

29 Correct the sentences.

1 Butterflies taste with their tongues.
2 Snakes and lizards smell with their legs.
3 To taste, bats use their ears.
4 Chameleons have got very short tongues.

I Can

- describe how things look, feel, taste, smell or sound.
- talk about the five senses in people and animals.
- find and use final sentences.

How Well Do I Know It? Can I Use It?

1 **Think about it. Read and draw. Practise.**

😊 I know this.   😐 I need more practice.   🙁 I don't know this.

		PAGES			
1	**Animals:** deer, owl, camel, lizard…	44	😊	😐	🙁
2	**Habitats:** lake, ocean, rainforest…	45	😊	😐	🙁
3	**Weather:** hot, cold, windy, rainy…	56	😊	😐	🙁
4	**Clothes:** coat, jumper, scarf…	57	😊	😐	🙁
5	**Describing:** awful, delicious, nice, pretty…	68	😊	😐	🙁
6	What **can** penguins do? They **can** swim but they **can't** fly. **Can** bears fly? No, they **can't**.	48–49	😊	😐	🙁
7	What is the weather like **today**? **It's** hot and sunny. What **was** the weather like **yesterday**? It **was** warm and windy last Sunday. It **wasn't** sunny. We **weren't** hot.	60–61	😊	😐	🙁
8	How **does** the apple pie **taste**? It **tastes** delicious. How **do** your new shoes **feel**? They **feel** good.	72–73	😊	😐	🙁

2 **Get ready.**

2:53

A Complete the dialogue. Use the words from the box. Then listen and check.

awful cold fly
look swim

Morgan: Look at those penguins!

Taylor: They ¹ 🔲 cool!

Morgan: Yeah. I like penguins. Hey, look at this: "Penguins live in the snow and ice."

Taylor: That sounds ² 🔲 !

Morgan: Yes, very cold. Listen. "They eat fish every day." Look. They're eating fish now!

Taylor: Yuck! That looks ³ 🔲 to me!

Morgan: Well, the penguins like it.

Taylor: Hey, look. They're swimming.

Morgan: Yes, penguins can ⁴ 🔲 . But they can't ⁵ 🔲 .

Taylor: Wow. I'm learning a lot about penguins!

B Practise the dialogue in **A** with a partner. Then practise again. Talk about different animals.

C Choose the words for you.
1 I **like/don't like** penguins.
2 Their food looks **delicious/terrible** to me.
3 Their home looks **warm/cold** to me.

3 **Get set.**

 STEP 1 Look and read. Find out information about an animal.

 STEP 2 Cut out the book outline on page 123 of your Activity Book. Fold it to make a book.

 STEP 3 Write in your own animal information book. Now you're ready to **Go!**

4 **Go!**

A Swap books with five classmates. Write notes about their books in your notebook.

Classmate	Animal	Comment
Carla	lizards	great

B Tell the class about some of your classmates' books.

Abby's book was about sharks. Sharks are amazing!

5 **Write about yourself in your notebook.**

- What was the weather like today?
- What was the weather like yesterday?
- Today I can...
- Today I can't...

- Today the sky looks...
- My classroom feels...
- My favourite animal is...
- I like this animal because...

All About Me Date:

_____

_____

How Well Do I Know It Now?

6 **Think about it. Look at page 80 and your notebook. Draw again.**

A **Use a different colour.**

B **Read and think.**

I can start the next unit.

I can ask my teacher for help and then start the next unit.

I can practise and then start the next unit.

7 **Rate this Checkpoint.**

very easy   easy   hard   very hard   fun   OK   not fun

1
2
3
4
5
6
7
8
9

Fabulous Food!

3:01

1 **Listen, look and say.**

At *Your Way Café* you decide what to put in your sandwich or on your pizza. There are so many things to choose from. Which will you choose?

1 Super Sandwiches!

2 cucumbers

3 turkey

1 bread

4 mustard

5 lettuce

2 Pizza Perfection!

6 green peppers

7 mushrooms

8 tomato sauce

9 olives

10 onions

3:02

2 **Listen, find and say.**

3 **Play a game.**

4 **Listen and sing. What do they eat?**

I'm Hungry!

Hi, Mum, I'm home from school.
I'm really hungry now.
I'd like to make a sandwich,
Can you show me how?

I am home from my school day.
I'd like a sandwich. Is that OK?

Are there any olives?
Here are some on the shelf.
Is there any tomato sauce?
I see it for myself.

Chorus

There's just one problem, Mum
There isn't any bread!
But I've got a great idea:
Let's have pizza instead!

Chorus

5 **Look at 1. Ask and answer.**

What do you like in your
sandwiches?

I like turkey and lettuce.

 What is good on pizzas and in sandwiches?

3:06

6 Listen and read. What are Luke and Amy making?

A Surprise for Mum

Are there any tomatoes for the pizza?

I can't see any but there's some cheese.

1 Luke and Amy are making dinner for their mum. It's a surprise.

Are there any onions?

No, there aren't. But there's a green pepper.

2 They need toppings for their pizza.

This cheese is yummy.

Mmm. These olives taste delicious, too!

3 Amy and Luke taste some of the pizza toppings.

Oh, no! There isn't any more cheese.

And there aren't any more olives. Oops.

4 They look in the fridge again. What can they use?

5 Amy and Luke look for more food.

6 There's a surprise for Mum in the kitchen but it isn't dinner.

7 **Read and say true or false.**

1 Amy and Luke want to make breakfast for their mother.
2 There aren't any onions for the pizza.
3 Amy and Luke eat all the cheese and olives.
4 There isn't any turkey.
5 There isn't a surprise for Mum.

THINK BIG **What do you think Amy and Luke's mum does next? Why? How can they help their mum?**

3:07

8 Listen and look at the sentences. Help Luke and Amy make more.

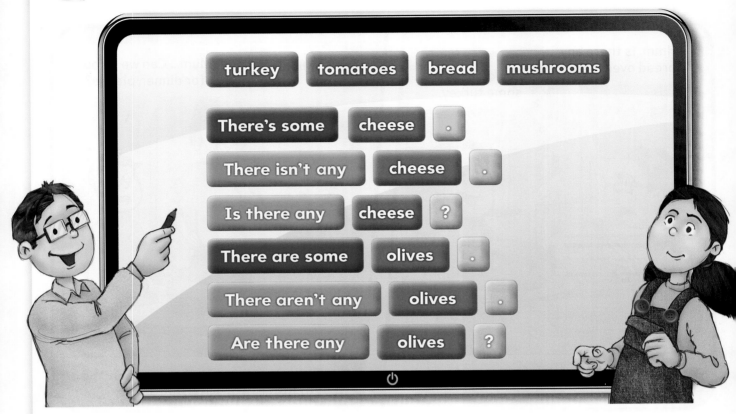

turkey tomatoes bread mushrooms

There's some cheese .

There isn't any cheese .

Is there any cheese ?

There are some olives .

There aren't any olives .

Are there any olives ?

9 Read and choose.

1 There's **some/any** tomato sauce on the pizza.

2 There are **some/any** sandwiches in my bag.

3 There aren't **some/any** olives in the kitchen.

4 There isn't **some/any** lettuce in my sandwich.

5 Are there **any/some** olives? Yes, there are.

6 **Is/Are** there any cheese? Yes, there is.

10 Make the questions.

1 No, there isn't. There isn't any bread.

2 Yes, there are some bananas. I think there are four.

3 Yes, there is. The lettuce is in the fridge.

4 No, there aren't any mushrooms in the soup. Don't worry!

5 Yes, there are some strawberries. They are next to the mangoes.

3:09

11 **Complete the dialogue in pairs. Then listen and check.**

Rob: Mum, can we have pizza for dinner?

Mum: Good idea. Look in the fridge. Is there ¹ 🔑 tomato sauce?

Rob: Yes, there ² 🔑 .

Mum: Is ³ 🔑 any cheese?

Rob: Yes, there is. There are ⁴ 🔑 mushrooms and some onions.

Mum: Great! What about olives? ⁵ 🔑 there ⁶ 🔑 olives?

Rob: No, there ⁷ 🔑 .

Mum: That's OK, Dad doesn't like olives. We can have pizza for dinner.

Rob: Brilliant. Let's start now.

12 **Look and make sentences in pairs. There is the food in blue and there isn't the food in red.**

bananas   bread   cheese   cucumbers   lettuce   mushrooms

There's...

... some cheese.

13 **Look. Ask and answer about the sandwich.**

Is there any turkey for your sandwich?

Yes, there is.

Are there any mushrooms for your sandwich?

No, there aren't.

3:10

14 Look, listen and repeat.

blood   bone   brain   energy   muscle   skin   teeth   vitamin

3:11

15 Listen and read. How do vitamins help us?

The Vitamin Alphabet

Vitamins help our bodies grow strong and stay healthy. We need vitamins every day. How do we get them?

	What It Does	**Where We Get It**
Vitamin A	Vitamin A is good for our eyes and skin. It helps them stay healthy.	We get this vitamin from carrots, mangoes, milk and eggs.
Vitamin B	There are many different kinds of Vitamin B. Some help give us energy to move. Others help make blood.	We get the different kinds of Vitamin B from different kinds of food. These include potatoes, bananas, bread, rice, pasta, chicken, fish, cheese, eggs and green peppers.
Vitamin C	Vitamin C is good for our bones, teeth and even our brains.	We get this vitamin from oranges, peppers, tomatoes and potatoes.
Vitamin D	Vitamin D helps make strong bones.	We get this vitamin from eggs, fish, milk – and even the sun, too!
Vitamin E	Vitamin E helps keep our blood healthy.	There is Vitamin E in nuts and green vegetables.

THINK BIG Which vitamins do the following people need and why? What food should they eat?

a a football player   **b** a pilot

16 **Read again and answer.**

1 What is Vitamin A good for?
2 Which vitamin do we get from bananas?
3 What is Vitamin C good for?
4 Which vitamin do we get from the sun?
5 Where do we get Vitamin E from?

17 **Where do you get vitamins from? Complete the chart. Tell your partner.**

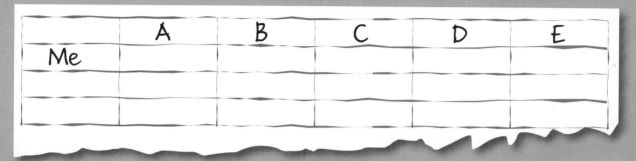

	A	B	C	D	E
Me					

PROJECT

18 **Make a Vitamin Plate. Then present it to the class.**

I've got carrots on my plate.
We get Vitamin A from carrots.
It's good for our skin.

3:13

19 **Listen and read. Which breakfast looks good to you? Why?**

Breakfast in Different Countries

Breakfast is a great way to start the day. Kids around the world eat many different things for breakfast. Here are just a few examples:

Japan

My name is Yoko. I'm from Japan. In the morning, I usually eat rice, soup, fish and pickles.

Spain

I'm Luis and I'm from Spain. I usually eat bread or cereal for breakfast but sometimes I eat churros with chocolate. Churros are like little doughnuts. They're delicious!

Mexico

My name is Camila. I'm from Mexico. For breakfast, I often eat huevos rancheros – fried eggs on toasted tortillas with salsa. They are spicy, colourful and delicious!

Australia

My name's Tony. I live in Australia. I like eating toast in the morning – with beans on top! Yum!

20 **Read and match the breakfast to the country. Then say.**

Australia	Japan	Mexico	Spain

doughnuts	fried eggs on toasted tortillas	rice and soup	beans on toast

In Australia, Tony lik[e] eating beans on toa[st] for breakfast.

 THINK BIG **What do people eat for breakfast in your country? Where do people eat these for breakfast? Find out!**

a kippers **b** kimchi **c** potato scones

3:14

 21 **Listen and read. Then match.**

> **Title** – says what you are writing about
> **Topic sentence** – explains the main idea
> **Detail sentences** – add more information
> **Final sentence** – summarises and gives an opinion

> detail sentences   final sentence   title   topic sentence

1 # My Favourite Breakfast
by Laura Brown

2 I like a lot of different things for breakfast but I have my favourite breakfast every Sunday morning.

3 I start with some orange slices, cold from the fridge. Then my mother makes two fluffy pancakes for me. I put butter on them and then I put warm maple syrup on top. The pancakes are delicious with a glass of cold milk.

4 My favourite breakfast makes Sundays special.

Writing Steps

22 **Write about your favourite breakfast.**

1 Think about your favourite breakfast.
2 Write a title.
3 Write a topic sentence.
4 Add details to give more information.
5 Write a final sentence.

23 Listen, read and repeat.

1 br **2** cr **3** dr **4** fr **5** gr **6** pr **7** tr

24 Listen and find. Then say.

bread **cream** **dream** **frog**

grass **prize** **train**

25 Listen and blend the sounds.

1 d-r-i-ve	drive	**2** g-r-ee-n	green
3 b-r-ow-n	brown	**4** p-r-i-n-ce	prince
5 c-r-y	cry	**6** t-r-o-ll	troll
7 f-r-o-m	from	**8** b-r-i-ck	brick

26 Read aloud. Then listen and chant.

Every night,
I dream
About a prince
And a troll
And a green frog!
In my dream,
They eat bread
With cream.

27 **Match the sentences.**

1 Vitamin C is good
2 Vitamin D helps
3 We get Vitamin A from
4 We get Vitamin D
5 Vitamin B gives us

a from the sun.
b energy and makes blood.
c for our bones, teeth and brains.
d carrots, milk and eggs.
e make strong bones.

28 **Read and choose. Then role play.**

Tina: Hi, Mum. I'm really hungry. Can I have a snack, please?
Mum: Have some fruit.
Tina: **Is/Are** there any strawberries?
Mum: I don't think so.
Tina: Is there **any/some** pineapple?
Mum: No, there isn't. What about an apple?
Tina: Is there any **cheese/olives**?
Mum: Yes, there **is/isn't**.
Tina: Great. A cheese sandwich!
Mum: Sorry, but there **isn't/aren't** any bread.
Tina: Well, I think I'll have an apple then.

29 **Make a pizza. Ask and answer to find two people with the same pizza. Use the words in the box.**

> cheese   chicken   cucumbers   mushrooms   olives
> onion   peppers   tomato sauce   turkey

Is there any cheese on your pizza?

Yes, there is.

I Can

- ask and answer about food.
- talk about vitamins and how they help my body.
- find different parts of a paragraph.

Unit 8 Healthy Living

3:20

1 Listen, look and say.

How do you feel today? Find out how healthy Sally and Zach are, then ask yourself!

I feel great today.

1 Did she... have a big breakfast?

5 Did he... eat breakfast?

2 Did she... get 10 hours sleep last night?

6 Did he... get any exercise?

3 Did she... drink lots of water?

7 Did he... have a healthy lunch?

4 Did she... ride her bike?

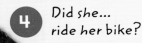

8 Did he... get enough sleep?

3:21

2 Listen, find and say.

3 Play a game.

4 **Listen and sing. How does Zach feel today?**

Live Right!

♪ Did you eat breakfast? asks Mum,
You don't look good to me.
Did you get enough sleep? asks Mum,
Did you watch too much TV?

Enough sleep. Good food.
Be healthy. Live right!
Enough sleep. Good food.
Be healthy. Live right!

Did you ride your bike? asks Mum,
You know it's good for you.
Did you get any exercise?
You know it's good to do!

Chorus

I feel awful today.

5 **Look at 1. Ask and answer.**

Did he eat breakfast?

Did she ride her bike?

No, he didn't.

Yes, she did.

THINK BIG **Which child in 1 are you like? Explain why.**

3:25
6 Listen and read. Did Amy eat a healthy dinner?

An Unhealthy Dinner

How was the party?

Uh...

Did you eat healthy food?

Kind of...

1 Amy's dad wants her to be healthy.

Well, did you eat any vegetables?

Yes, I did. I ate two burgers. They had onions and tomato ketchup on them. Onions and tomatoes are vegetables!

2 Amy likes unhealthy food.

Yes, I suppose so.

And I ate lots of chips. Chips are potatoes. They are vegetables, aren't they?

3 Amy likes chips but fried food isn't very healthy.

Did you drink any water?

No, I didn't. I drank a large cola.

4 Amy likes cola.

5 Amy knows her dinner wasn't really healthy. She didn't eat many vegetables.

6 Now Amy doesn't feel well. She needs to eat healthy food.

7 **Read and choose.**

1 Amy had dinner at a **party/home**.
2 Amy likes **healthy/unhealth**y food.
3 Chips are fried **potatoes/onions**.
4 Fried food is **good/bad** for you.
5 Cola has got a lot of **fruit/sugar** in it.
6 Amy's dad **is/isn't** happy about Amy's dinner.

THINK BIG **What should Amy eat for her next dinner? Why?**

3:26

8 Listen and look at the sentences. Help Luke and Amy make more.

| drink lots of water | eat a healthy lunch |
| get enough exercise |

Did you have breakfast ?

No , I didn't .

Did he get enough sleep ?

Yes , he did .

9 Match the phrases. Make five questions about yesterday.
Then ask and answer.

1	do any	**a**	of water
2	drink lots	**b**	healthy lunch
3	have a	**c**	sleep
4	get enough	**d**	my bike
5	ride	**e**	exercise

Did you do any
exercise yesterday?

No, I didn't.

10 **Complete the dialogues. Use did or didn't.**

1 **A:** Good morning, Katia. 🔔 you eat breakfast?

   B: Yes, I 🔔 .

2 **A:** 🔔 Ted take a shower this morning?

   B: No, he 🔔 .

3 **A:** 🔔 the football team get enough sleep before the game?

   B: No, they 🔔 .

4 **A:** 🔔 Melissa brush her teeth?

   B: Yes, she 🔔 .

11 **Put the words in order to make questions. Then ask.**

1 yesterday? | Did | get | enough | Alice | sleep

2 play football | last week? | Did | after school | they

3 a shower | Did | have | this morning? | you

4 play | video games | weekend? | we | Did | at the

5 on Sunday? | go | Matthew | Did | to the park

12 **Read and match. Now change the answers.**

1 Did Ruth visit her cousin yesterday?

2 Did you go to a national park?

3 Did Mike like the band?

4 Did your mum and dad watch a DVD?

5 Did Melanie have onions on her pizza?

6 Did you learn a lot at school today?

a Yes, they did. It was great.

b Yes, I did. I learned about healthy and unhealthy food.

c No, she didn't. She hates them!

d Yes, she did. She was glad to see her.

e No, he didn't. He doesn't like going to concerts.

f No, we didn't. It was too cold and snowy.

3:28

13 **Look, listen and repeat.**

active   activities   body   calorie   measure   put on weight

3:29

14 **Listen and read. What is a calorie?**

What Is a Calorie?

A calorie is a measure of the energy you get from food. Your body needs a certain number of calories to do all the things you do every day. But if you eat more calories than your body needs, you can put on too much weight.

Being Active is Important!

Being active is really important whether you are young or old. Did you know that some activities are better for you than others? Dancing is really good for your body. Riding a bike and swimming are also good for your body. Sleeping is good for your health but sleeping too much is definitely bad for you. How many hours a night do you sleep? What about watching TV or playing video games? They are bad for your health if you do them too much. How much time do you spend in front of the TV or computer? Paying attention to what exercise you do can help you stay fit.

THINK BIG **Which activities do you spend most of your time doing?**
watching TV   eating   playing a sport
playing computer games   sleeping   riding a bike

15 Look at 14. Complete the chart. Add more.

> dancing   riding my bike to school   playing a sport   playing video games
> sleeping for 13 hours   watching TV

Good for your body	Bad for your body

16 Make false sentences. Then correct.

Running is bad for my body.

False! Running is good for your body.

PROJECT

17 Make an **Exercise Chart** for you. Then present it to the class.

Activity	Hours a week	Hours a month	Hours a year
Dancing	4	16	192

I love dancing. Dancing is good for your health. I go to dance classes twice a week. I dance for 4 hours a week, 16 hours a month and 192 hours a year!

3:30

18 **Listen and read. How many sports are there?**

Strange Sports

Almost everyone knows about football, baseball and basketball. But do you know anything about octopush, footvolley or pumpkin regattas? Read about these strange sports!

Octopush

Octopush comes from England but people now play it all over the world. Octopush is like hockey but people play it under water. Players use a small stick. They try to push a puck into a net to score points for their team.

Footvolley

Footvolley is a sport from Brazil. Footvolley is like volleyball but the players use a football. Players have to pass the ball to the other team over a high net. They can't touch the ball with their hands. People play footvolley on the beach. It's very exciting but very difficult!

Pumpkin Regatta

In autumn, in parts of the United States and Canada, people join in a contest called a pumpkin regatta. It's like a boat race but the players don't race in boats. They race in giant, hollowed out pumpkins! These pumpkins weigh more than 450 kilograms. After the race, there's a pumpkin pie-eating contest.

19 **Read and say true or false. Correct the false sentences.**

1 Octopush is from England.

2 Hockey isn't like octopush.

3 You need a net and a football to play footvolley.

4 You throw the ball over the net for points.

5 A Pumpkin Regatta is popular in America and Canada.

THINK BIG **Which of these three strange sports sound fun to you?**

20 **Complete these sentences. Then listen and check.**

> I go to bed at 9:00 and wake up at 7:00.
> Dad eats cheese but Mum doesn't eat cheese.
> We can go to the park or go to the cinema.

and but or

1 I like eating olives ❓ I don't like eating tomatoes.
2 I never clean my room ❓ take out the rubbish.
3 I get dressed at 7:15 ❓ I go to school at 8:30.

21 **Join these sentences. Then write.**

1 My sister plays tennis. My brother plays baseball. (*and*)
2 I usually eat eggs in the morning. This morning, I'm having pancakes. (*but*)
3 We can have chicken for dinner. We can try the new restaurant. (*or*)
4 There aren't any onions in the fridge. There are some green peppers. (*but*)
5 My dad works at a hospital. My mum works at a school. (*and*)

22 **Read and choose.**

I don't like playing sports **but/or** I need to get some exercise. I usually play video games after school **but/or** I watch a DVD. My sister likes playing tennis **and/but** volleyball but I don't. But I love going hiking with my family in the mountains. It's cool to see lots of animals **and/but** birds.

23 **Write three sentences about healthy habits. Use and, but and or once.**

3:32

24 **Listen, read and repeat.**

1 all   **2** au   **3** aw

 3:33

25 **Listen and find. Then say.**

b**all**   h**au**l   dr**aw**

 3:34

26 **Listen and blend the sounds.**

1	s-m-all	small	**2**	c-all	call
3	t-all	tall	**4**	y–aw-n	yawn
5	c-l-aw	claw	**6**	w-all	wall
7	l-aw	law	**8**	P-aul	Paul

 3:35

27 **Read aloud. Then listen and chant.**

I'm Paul, I'm bored.
Yawn, yawn.
Let's play, let's play
With a ball,
Let's draw, let's draw
A wall.

28 **Read and choose. Then say.**

1 Did she **eat**/**eating** a fruit salad at lunchtime?
2 **Did/Don't** you do any exercise yesterday?
3 Did they drink lots of water today? No, they **did**/**didn't**.
4 Lenny is tired. He **didn't**/**don't** get enough sleep last night.

29 **Do a survey of your classmates. Add two of your own questions. Ask and answer.**

1 eat/healthy/food?
2 get/sleep/last night?
3 do/exercise/last week?
4 brush/teeth/this morning?
5 ride/bike/at the weekend?
6 drink/lots/water/today?
7 ?
8 ?

Did you get enough sleep last night?

Yes, I did.

30 **Write the answers.**

1 Did you get enough sleep last night?
2 Did you get any exercise last weekend?
3 Did you eat a healthy breakfast this morning?
4 Did you drink enough water yesterday?
5 Did your mum or dad get a lot of sleep last night?
6 Did your friend play tennis last month?
7 Did your teacher eat an unhealthy dinner yesterday?

I Can

• talk about healthy and unhealthy habits.
• ask and answer about activities in the past.
• use *and*, *or* and *but* in sentences.

Unit 9 School Trips!

3:37

1 Listen, look and say.

Top **8** places to visit!

1 museum

2 dairy farm

3 art gallery

4 national park

5 theatre

6 zoo

7 concert hall

8 aquarium

3:38

2 Listen, find and say.

3 Play a game.

4 **Listen and sing. Did she visit the zoo?**

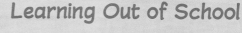

Learning Out of School

I like going on school trips,
Learning out of school.
We go to lots of places.
They're interesting and cool!

Aquarium, theatre, concert hall and zoo,
We saw some great things.
There was lots to do!

School trips. School trips.
They're a lot of fun.
School trips. School trips.
Let's go on one!

Where did you go?
What did you see?
We went to the zoo, we saw a play,
We had a great time!

Chorus

Zoo
ADMIT ONE

5 **Look at 1. Ask and answer.**

It was a
sunny day.

Yes, I did.

Did you go to a
national park?

THINK BIG **Why is it good to go on school trips?**

Story

Listen and read. Did Luke enjoy the trip?

A Cool Trip

1 Amy and Luke went on a trip today.

2 They went to a big park where there are very old rocks.

3 Their guide told them a lot of things about the rocks in the park.

4 Amy liked the park.

5 Luke didn't like the trip. He didn't like walking a lot.

6 Luke doesn't want to see another rock!

7 **Read and answer.**

1 Where did Luke and Amy go on their trip?

2 What did they learn about?

3 Did Amy like the trip? Why/Why not?

4 Did Luke enjoy the trip? Why/Why not?

5 What did Amy get for Luke in the gift shop?

THINK BIG What national parks are there in your country? Why have we got national parks?

3:43

8 Listen and look at the sentences. Help Luke and Amy make more.

| got | had | liked | learned |

Where did | he | go | ?

He | went | to an aquarium | .

What did | they | do | ?

They | walked | a lot | .

They | didn't see | a penguin | .

9 Complete the chart. Then make new sentences.

did (x2)   didn't   go   saw   went

1	Where	did	they	🔾	?	They	went	to the zoo.
2	What	🔾	she	do	?	She	🔾	a play.
3		Did	you	like it	?	Yes, I	🔾	
4		Did	you	go to the museum	?	No, I	🔾 go	to the museum.

Did you go to the zoo yesterday?

No, I didn't.

10 **Match the verbs. Test your partner. Then make sentences.**

1 go   **a** ate
2 have   **b** saw
3 get   **c** had
4 eat   **d** went
5 is   **e** got
6 see   **f** was

go went We went to the theatre yesterday.

11 **Use the verbs from 10 in the past. Then say.**

1 Yesterday, I ❓ two bananas before school.
2 Susie ❓ you a present from the gift shop.
3 At the weekend, I ❓ a play at the theatre.
4 The school trip ❓ great.
5 We ❓ a lot of fun on our trip to the zoo.
6 They ❓ to a national park on Friday.

12 **Ask and answer. Use the words in the boxes.**

last weekend   last year   yesterday

eat   go   get   have   is   learn   like   see   visit   walk

Where did you go yesterday?

I went to the art gallery. It was fun.

13 Look, listen and repeat.

> beautiful   boring   colourful   funny   interesting   scary   strange

14 Listen and look. Which painting is by a French artist?

At the Art Gallery

1 *The Little Giants* by Francisco de Goya

2 *Nature and Fantasy* by Giuseppe Arcimboldo

3 *Old Man with his Head in his Hands* by Vincent Van Gogh

4 *Haystacks at Giverny* by Claude Monet

 What do you like most in paintings: the colours, the people or the things? Why?

15 Match the countries to the nationalities.

Spain	America		Italian	French
Italy	England		Spanish	Turkish
China	France		English	American
The Netherlands	Turkey		Dutch	Chinese

3:47

16 Can you remember? Listen and check.

1 Is painting number 1 by a Spanish artist?

2 Is painting number 2 by an Italian artist?

3 Is painting number 3 by an English artist?

4 Is painting number 4 by a Chinese artist?

17 Ask and answer.

I saw a painting by Van Gogh. It's called *The Old Man with his Head in his Hands.*

No, I didn't. It was scary.

Did you like it?

PROJECT

18 Find out about a famous painting. Then present it to the class.

I went to the National Gallery in London. It's a famous art gallery. I saw a painting by George Stubbs. It is called *Whistlejacket.* I loved the horse. I think it's a beautiful painting because I love animals.

3:48

19 Listen and read. What is popular in Vietnam?

The World Stage

Today, people everywhere enjoy watching films and television. But before films and television, people went to the theatre to see plays. Here are a few different kinds of theatre from around the world.

Flamenco

Flamenco is a kind of dance from Spain. It started hundreds of years ago but people still enjoy watching and performing flamenco today. Flamenco music and dance are very dramatic. Together, the music and dance tell a story.

Mua Roi Nuoc

In Vietnam, there's an interesting kind of theatre called *Mua Roi Nuoc*. There are no actors – only puppets. The puppets are on a stage filled with water. Mua Roi Nuoc started hundreds of years ago but people still enjoy watching the shows today.

Shakespeare's Plays

William Shakespeare wrote many plays in England about 400 years ago. You can see his plays all over the world today. One of his most famous plays is *Romeo and Juliet*. In the 1600s, Shakespeare's plays were very popular. In those days, all of the parts were played by men.

20 Read and say true or false.

1 People dance flamenco in Vietnam.

2 Flamenco isn't a new dance.

3 There are many actors in Mua Roi Nuoc.

4 There are puppets and water in the show.

5 Shakespeare's plays aren't popular.

THINK BIG Which do you prefer watching: dance, theatre or films? Why?

21 **Read and find. Then listen and check.**

Sentences have got subjects, verbs and objects. They appear in this order:

We had fun.

They didn't see a show.

Did you see a sea lion show?

1 Did you visit a zoo?

2 Yes, I did.

3 I saw elephants and zebras.

22 **Find the subjects, verbs and objects.**

1 Did she visit a dairy farm?

2 They didn't see any scary paintings.

3 I learned about rocks.

4 Did you see a film?

23 **Put the words in order to make detail sentences.**

1 went   We   to the National Gallery.

2 old and new paintings.   saw   I

3 love   I   painting and listening to guides.

4 Our class   famous artists.   learned about

24 **Find the title, topic sentence and final sentence. Now write the paragraph in your notebook.**

It was lots of fun.   My favourite school trip
We usually go on school trips every summer.

3:50

25 **Listen, read and repeat.**

1 nt   **2** ld   **3** nd   **4** st

3:51

26 **Listen and find. Then say.**

ten**t**   **chi**l**d**   **ha**n**d**   **ne**s**t**

3:52

27 **Listen and blend the sounds.**

1 p-l-a-n-t   plant   **2** o-l-d   old
3 c-o-l-d   cold   **4** b-a-n-d   band
5 s-a-n-d   sand   **6** a-n-t   ant
7 ch-e-s-t   chest   **8** f-a-s-t   fast

3:53

28 **Read aloud. Then listen and chant.**

An old, cold band
Playing in the sand.
A fast ant
Playing in a tent.

29 **Look and say the places.**

1  **2**  **3**  **4**

30 **Complete the dialogue. Then role play.**

A: Hey! How are you, Susie?

B: I'm fine, Dad.

A: What did you ¹ 🔊 today?

B: I ² 🔊 on a school trip with my class.

A: Cool! Where ³ 🔊 you ⁴ 🔊 ?

B: We went to the ⁵ 🔊 .

A: That sounds fun. Did you ⁶ 🔊 it?

B: Yes. I ⁷ 🔊 . It ⁸ 🔊 really fun!

31 **Work with a partner. Plan your own school trip. Then present it to the class.**

Where did you go?

What did you do?

What did you learn?

Did you like it?

Why/Why not?

We went to a toy museum. We saw some very old toys. Some of them were a hundred years old! We liked it a lot.

I Can

- talk about actions in the past and places to visit.
- talk about paintings.
- write sentences with a subject, verb and object.

Checkpoint | Units 7–9

How Well Do I Know It? Can I Use It?

1 **Think about it. Read and draw. Practise.**

🙂 I know this.   😐 I need more practice.   🙁 I don't know this.

		PAGES			
1	**Food:** bread, mustard, onions, turkey...	84	🙂	😐	🙁
2	**Healthy habits:** ate breakfast, drank water, got enough sleep, rode my bike...	96	🙂	😐	🙁
3	**School trip places:** aquarium, museum, national park, theatre...	108	🙂	😐	🙁
4	**School trip activities:** saw a penguin show, saw a film, learned about rocks, saw a play...	109	🙂	😐	🙁
5	**Is** there **any** pizza? Yes, there is./No, there isn't. There**'s some** pizza. **Are** there **any** mushrooms? Yes, there are./No, there aren't. There are **some** mushrooms.	88–89	🙂	😐	🙁
6	**Did** you **get** enough exercise? Yes, I **did**. **Did** you **get** enough sleep? No, I **didn't**.	100–101	🙂	😐	🙁
7	Where **did** they **go**? They **went** to the zoo. What **did** they **see**? They **saw** a parrot show. **Did** they **like** it? Yes, they did.	112–113	🙂	😐	🙁

I Can Do It!

3:55

2 **Get ready.**

A Complete the dialogue with Kelly's answers. Then listen and check.

Kelly: Hello?

Dad: Hi, Kelly. It's Dad.

Kelly: Oh, hi, Dad!

Dad: How is New York City?

Kelly: 1 ❓

Dad: What did you do yesterday?

Kelly: 2 ❓

Dad: That sounds fun. Did you like it?

Kelly: 3 ❓

Dad: Great. So, when is your football game?

Kelly: 4 ❓

Dad: I see. Did you get enough sleep last night?

Kelly: 5 ❓

Dad: That's good. Did you eat breakfast this morning?

Kelly: 6 ❓

Dad: That sounds delicious! Well, good luck today. Call me after your game.

Kelly: OK, Dad. Talk to you later.

Dad: Bye.

Kelly's answers

a Yes, Dad. I ate a big pancake.

b Yes, it was great! We saw a lot of interesting paintings.

c Yes, I went to bed at 7:00 last night.

d We went to the Museum of Modern Art.

e It's today. It starts at 2:00.

f It's really cool. We arrived yesterday afternoon.

1

2

3

4

5

6

7

8

9

B Practise the dialogue in **A** with a partner. Make up your own answers.

3 **Get set.**

STEP 1 Cut out the cards on page 125 of your Activity Book.

STEP 2 Read Dialogue 1 below. Then place the cards in order to create Dialogue 2.

STEP 3 Look at the pictures below. Choose the picture that illustrates each dialogue. Now you're ready to **Go!**

4 **Go!**

A With a partner, practise Dialogue 1. Change parts and practise again.

A: Where did you go yesterday?

B: We went to a big art gallery.

A: What did you do there?

B: We looked at some paintings.

A: Did you like it?

B: Not really. The paintings were strange.

A: What did you eat for dinner?

B: I ate a big pizza. It was delicious.

A: Did you get enough sleep last night?

B: No. I went to bed at 11:00.

A: Did you eat breakfast this morning?

B: No. I drank some water. I feel a bit ill.

Where did you go yesterday?

We went to a big art gallery.

B Use your cards to act out Dialogue 2 with a partner.

5 **Write about yourself in your notebook.**

- Where did you go last weekend?

- What did you do there?

- Did you like it?

- What or Who did you see?

- Did you get enough sleep last night?

- Did you eat a healthy breakfast?

- Did you get any exercise?

All About Me   Date:

_____

_____

How Well Do I Know It Now?

6 **Think about it. Look at page 120 and your notebook. Draw again.**

A **Use a different colour.**

B **Read and think.**

I can ask my teacher for help.

I can practise.

7 **Rate this Checkpoint.**

very easy   easy   hard   very hard   fun   OK   not fun

1

2

3

4

5

6

7

8

9

Wordlist

Find these words in your language. Then write in your notebook.

Unit 1	Page
do my homework	4
eat breakfast	4
get dressed	4
go home	4
go to school	4
go to the park	4
home	4
play football	4
play video games	4
wake up	4
watch TV	4
seven thirty	5
time	5
brush your teeth	6
face	6
morning	6
like	7
put on his shoes	7
afternoon	8
evening	8
game	8
seven fifty	8
bike	9
ride	9
bacteria	10
cough	10
decay	10
germ	10
have a shower	10

	Page
healthy	10
ill	10
sneeze	10
wash your hands	10
time zone	12
subject	13
verb	13
bone	14
cake	14
note	14
shape	14

Unit 2	Page
cashier	16
farmer	16
firefighter	16
nurse	16
police officer	16
scientist	16
student	16
waiter	16
farm	17
fire station	17
hospital	17
laboratory	17
police station	17
shop	17
university	17
school	20
fashion designer	22

	Page
gallery	22
landscape	22
photographer	22
sketch	22
upload	22
donate	24
proud	24
Spain	24
skates	26
ski	26
skin	26
smart	26
smile	26
smoke	26
space	26
spoon	26
star	26
stop	26
storm	26

Unit 3	Page
chores	28
clean my room	28
do the dishes	28
feed the fish	28
make my bed	28
practise the piano	28
study for a test	28
take out the rubbish	28
walk the dog	28

Wordlist

brick	94	pumpkin	104	beautiful	114
cream	94	race	104	boring	114
cry	94	throw	104	colourful	114
dream	94	claw	106	French	114
drive	94	draw	106	funny	114
frog	94	haul	106	hand	114
grass	94	tall	106	scary	114
prince	94	wall	106	strange	114
prize	94	yawn	106	Chinese	115
troll	94			Dutch	115
				English	115
Unit 8	**Page**	**Unit 9**	**Page**	Italian	115
healthy	96	aquarium	108	Spanish	115
any	97	art gallery	108	Flamenco	116
enough	97	concert hall	108	Vietnam	116
unhealthy	98	dairy farm	108	object	117
bad	99	museum	108	ant	118
active	102	national park	108	band	118
activities	102	school trip	108	chest	118
body	102	theatre	108	child	118
calorie	102	zoo	108	cold	118
measure	102	had	109	fast	118
put on weight	102	interesting	109	nest	118
all	102	saw	109	plant	118
ball	104	went	109	sand	118
call	104	learned	110	tent	118
footvolley	104	liked	110		
hockey	104	old	110		
net	104	got	111		
octopush	104	walked	111		
		ate	113		

Big English Song

From the mountaintops to the bottom of the sea,
From a big blue whale to a baby bumblebee-
If you're big, if you're small, you can have it all,
And you can be anything you want to be!

**It's bigger than you. It's bigger than me.
There's so much to do and there's so much to see!
The world is big and beautiful and so are we!
Think big! Dream big! Big English!**

So in every land, from the desert to the sea
We can all join hands and be one big family.
If we love, if we care, we can go anywhere!
The world belongs to everyone; it's ours to share.

**It's bigger than you. It's bigger than me.
There's so much to do and there's so much to see!
The world is big and beautiful and so are we!
Think big! Dream big! Big English!**

**It's bigger than you. It's bigger than me.
There's so much to do and there's so much to see!
The world is big and beautiful and waiting for me.
A One, two, three...
Think big! Dream big! Big English!**